Lev Tolstoy

Godson

Lev Tolstoy

Godson

ISBN/EAN: 9783337330620

Printed in Europe, USA, Canada, Australia, Japan

Cover: Foto ©Lupo / pixelio.de

More available books at **www.hansebooks.com**

The Godson

Lev Tolstoy

The Godson

By Lev Tolstoy

"You have heard that it has been said, an eye for an eye, and a tooth for a tooth: but I say unto you, that you resist no evil." (Matt. V. 38, 39.)

"Vengeance is mine, I will repay." (Rom. xii. 19).

I

A poor peasant had a son born to him. Greatly delighted, he went off to a neighbour's to ask him to stand godfather; but the neighbour refused, since he was unwilling to stand godfather to a poor man's son. Then the father went to another neighbour with the same request, but this man too refused.

In fact, the peasant made the round of the village, but no one would stand godfather, and he was driven to pursue his quest elsewhere. On the way to another village he fell in with a passer-by, who stopped when he met him.

- Good-day to you, friend peasant, - he said. - Where is God taking you?

- He has just given me a child, - replied the peasant, - that it may be a joy to me in my prime, a comfort to me in my old age, and a memorial to my soul when I am dead. Yet, because of my poverty, no one in our village will stand godfather, and I am just off to seek godparents elsewhere.

- Take myself as godfather, - said the stranger.

The peasant was delighted, and, thanking him for the offer, inquired:

- Whom, then, shall I ask to be godmother?

- A merchant's daughter whom I know, - replied the other. - Go to the town, to the stone building with the shops in it which fronts the square. Enter and ask the proprietor to give his daughter leave to stand godmother.

The peasant demurred to this.

- But, my good friend, - he said, - who am I that I should go and call upon a rich merchant? He will only turn away from me in disgust, and refuse his daughter leave.

- That will not be your fault. Go and ask him. - Arrange the christening for tomorrow morning, and I will be there.

So the poor peasant returned home, first of all, and then set out to the merchant's in the town. He was fastening up his horse in the courtyard when the merchant himself came out.

- What do you want? - he said.

- This, sir, -replied the peasant, - God has just given to me a child, that it may be a joy to me in my prime, a comfort to me in my old age, and a memorial to my soul when I am dead. Pray give your daughter leave to stand godmother.

- When is the christening to be?

- Tomorrow morning.

- So be it. God go with you. Tomorrow my daughter will be at the christening Mass.

And, sure enough, on the following morning both the godfather and the godmother arrived, and the child was christened; but as soon as ever the christening was over, the godfather departed without revealing his identity, and they never saw him again.

II

The child grew up to be a delight to his parents, for he was strong, hardworking, smart and obedient. When he was ten years old his parents sent him to learn his letters, and he learnt in a year what others took five years to master. And they could teach him nothing else.

One Holy Week the boy went as usual to visit his godmother and give her the Easter embrace, then he had returned home and asked:

- Dear father and mother, where does my godfather live? I should like to go and give him the Easter greeting.

But the father said to him:

- We do not know, beloved son, where your godfather lives. We ourselves have often been troubled about that. Never since the day of your christening have we set eyes upon him, nor heard of him; so that we neither know where he lives nor whether he be alive at all.

Then the boy knelt down before his father and mother.

- Let me go and look for him, dear father and mother, - he said. - I might find him and give him the Easter greeting.

So the father and mother let their boy go, and he went off searching for his godfather.

III

Leaving the home, the boy started along the highroad, and had been walking about half the day when he met a stranger.

The stranger stopped.

- Good-day to you, little boy, - he said. - Where is God taking you?

- This morning, - answered the boy, - I went to visit my godmother and give her the Easter greeting, after which I returned home and asked my parents: "Where does my godfather live? I should like to go and give him also the Easter greeting." But my parents said to me: "Sonny, we do not know where your godfather lives. As soon as ever you had been christened he left our house, so that we know nothing about him nor whether he be alive at all." Yet I felt a great longing to see my godfather, and now have come out to seek him.

Then the stranger said:

- I am your godfather.

The boy was overjoyed, and straightway gave his godfather the Easter embrace.

- But where are you going now, dear godfather? - He asked. - If in our direction, come with me to our hut; and if to your own home, let me come with you.

And his godfather replied:

- Nay, I have no time now to go to your home, for I have business to do in the villages; but I shall be back at my own home tomorrow, and you may come to me then.

- And how shall I find the way to you, dear godfather?

- Walk straight towards the rising sun, and you will come to a forest, and in the middle of the forest to a clearing. Sit down there and rest yourself, and observe what happens in that spot. Then come out of the forest, and you will see in front of you a garden, and in that garden a pavilion with a golden roof to it. That is my home. Walk straight up to the garden gates; and I will meet you there.

Thus spoke the godfather, and then vanished from his godson's eyes.

IV

So the boy went by the way that his godfather had told him. On and on he went, until he reached the forest, and then a little open field in the middle of it. In the centre of this field stood a pine tree, to one branch of which a rope was fastened, and to the other end of the rope an oaken log some fifty kilograms. Exactly beneath the log there was placed a pail of honey. Just as the boy was wondering why the honey had been put there, there came a crackling sound from the forest, and he saw some bears approaching. In front walked the mother bear, behind her a young yearling bear, and behind him again three little bear cubs. The mother bear raised her muzzle and sniffed, and then made straight for the pail, with the young ones behind her. First she plunged her own nose into the pail, and then called the young ones. Up they ran, and fell to work on the honey; but their doing so caused the log to swing a little, and to thrust the cubs away as it swung back. Seeing this, the old she-bear pushed it away again with her paw. It swung further this time, and, returning, struck two of the cubs—one of them on the head, and the other one on the back—so that they squealed and jumped aside. This angered the mother bear, and, raising both paws to the log, she lifted it above her head and flung it far away from her. High up it swung, and immediately the yearling bear leapt to the pail, buried his nose in the honey, and munched away greedily, while the cubs also began to return. Before, however, they had reached the pail the log came flying back, struck the yearling bear on the head, and killed him outright. The mother bear growled more fiercely than ever as she seized the log and flung it away from her with all her strength. Up, up it flew—higher than the branch itself, and well-nigh breaking the rope. Then the she-bear approached the pail, and the cubs after her. The log had gone flying upwards and upwards, but now it stopped, and began to descend. The lower it came, the faster it travelled. Faster and faster it flew, until it struck the mother bear and crashed against her head. She turned over, stretched out her paws, and died, while the cubs ran away.

V

The boy marvelled at what he saw, and then went on until he came to a large garden, in the middle of which stood a lofty pavilion with a golden roof to it. At the entrance gates of the garden stood his godfather smiling, who greeted his godson, drew him within, and led him through the grounds. Never, even in a dream, had the boy seen such beauty and delight as were contained in that garden.

Next, his godfather conducted him into the pavilion, the interior of which was even more beautiful than the garden had been. Through every room did his godfather lead him—each one more magnificent, more enchanting than the last—until he had brought him to a sealed door.

- Do you see this door? - He said. - There is no lock upon it - only seals. Yet, although it can be opened, I bid you not do so. You may live here and play here, where you like and how you like, and enjoy all these delights; but this one charge do I lay upon you - that you do not enter that door. If ever you should do so, you will remember what you have so lately seen in the forest.

Thus his godfather spoke, and disappeared. Left alone, his godson lived so happily and joyfully that he seemed only to have been there three hours when in reality he had been there thirty years. At the end of those thirty years the godson drew near to the sealed door and thought within himself, "Why did my godfather forbid me to enter that room? Suppose I go in now and see what it contains?"

So he pushed at the door, the seals parted, and the door flew open. As he entered he could see rooms larger and more splendid even than the others, and that in the midst of them there was set a golden throne. On and on he walked through those rooms, until he had come to the throne. Ascending the steps, he sat down upon it. Hardly had he done so when he perceived a sceptre resting against the throne. He took this sceptre into his hand—and lo! in a moment all the four walls of all the surrounding rooms had rolled away. He looked round him, and sees the whole world at a glance and all that people were doing in it. In front of him - he saw the sea and the ships sailing over it. To his right - he viewed the life of all foreign, non-Christian nations. To his left - he watched the doings of all Christian nations other than the Russian. And lastly, on the fourth side, - he observed how our own - the Russian - nation was living. "Let me see," - he said to himself, - "what is happening in my own home, and whether the crop has come up well?" So he looked towards his own native field, and saw sheaves (bunches of wheat) standing there; he began to count them, to see how many there were. While he was doing this, he caught sight of a cart going across the field, with a peasant sitting in it. At first he thought it must be his father going to carry sheaves home by night, but when he looked again he saw that it was Vassili Kudnishoff, the thief, who was driving the cart. Up to the sheaves he drove, and began to load them on to the cart. The godson was enraged at this, and cried out: Father dear! They are stealing sheaves from your field!"

His father awoke in the middle of the night. "Somehow I dreamt that my sheaves were being stolen," - he said. - "Let me go and look." So he mounted his horse and set off.

As soon as he came to the field, he saw Vassili there, and called men. Other peasants came, and Vassili was beaten, bound, and carried off to jail.

Next, the godson looked towards the town where his godmother was living, and saw that she was now married to a merchant. There she lay asleep, while her husband had got out of bed and was sneaking off to his paramour's room. So the godson cried out to the merchant's wife: "Arise! your husband is about an evil business."

His godmother leapt out of bed, dressed herself and went to look for her husband. She shamed him utterly, beat his paramour, and turned him out of doors.

Then the godson looked at his mother, and sees - while she was lying asleep, a robber entered the hut, and began to break open her chest.

At this moment she awoke and cried out, whereupon the robber seized a hatchet, flourished it over her, and wanted to kill her.

The godson could not restrain himself, but flung the sceptre towards the robber. Striking him right on the temple, killed him on the spot.

VI

Instantly when the godson had killed the robber, the walls of the pavilion closed in again, and the place became as before.

Then the door opened, and the godfather entered. He went up to his godson, and, taking him by the hand, led him down from the throne.

- You have not obeyed my command, - he said. - One thing you have done which you ought not: you have opened the forbidden door. A second thing you have done which you ought not: you have ascended the throne and taken my sceptre into your hands. And a third thing you have done which you ought not: you have caused much evil in the world. Had you sat there but another hour you would have ruined the half of mankind.

Then the godfather led his godson back to the throne, and took the sceptre into his hands. Once again the walls rolled back, and all the world became visible.

- Look now, what you have done to your father, - said the godfather. – By then, Vassili sat for a year in prison, and there he learnt every kind of villainy and became completely embittered against his fellow-man. Now, see, he has just stolen two of your father's horses, and is at this very moment in the act of firing his farm also. That is what you have done to your father.

Yet, as soon as the godson saw that his father's farm was caught by fire, his godfather closed that view from him and told him look in another direction.

- Look there, - he said. – It's already a year since the husband of your godmother has deserted her, now he leads a lustful five with others, and she has been driven by her grief to drink, and her husband's paramour is downright ruined. That is what you have done to your godmother.

Then godfather closed this picture from his godson and pointed toward the godson's own home. In it sat his mother, weeping tears of remorse for her sins and saying: "It would be better if I'd been killed by the robber, - for then I wouldn't have sinned that much."

- That is what you have done to your mother.

Then the godfather hid this view also from his godson, and pointed below it. There the godson saw the robber: standing before a dungeon, with two warders holding him.

And the godfather said to his godson:

- This man has taken nine lives. He would have had to atone his sins, but you have killed him, and now you have transferred those sins to yourself, and for them all you must answer. That is what you have done to yourself. Remember bear? The first time that the old she-bear pushed away the log, she only frightened her cubs a little. The second time that she pushed it away, she killed the yearling bear by doing so. But the third time that she pushed the log away, she killed herself. So also have you done. Yet I will set you now a term of thirty years in which to go forth into the world and atone for the sins of that robber. Should you not atone for them within that time, then it will be your fate to go where he has gone.

And the godson said:

- In what manner shall I atone for his sins?

To this the godfather replied:

- When you have relieved the world of as much evil as you have brought into it, then will you have atoned for the sins of that robber.

- But in what manner, - asked his godson again, - am I to relieve the world of evil?

And the godfather replied:

- Go you towards the rising sun, until you come to a field with men in it. Note carefully what those men do, and teach them what you yourself have learnt. Then go forward again, still noting what you see, and on the fourth day you will come to a forest. Within that forest there stands a hermit's cell, and in that cell an old man lives. Tell him all that has befallen you, and he will instruct you. When you have done all that he orders you to do, then will you have atoned both for the sins of that robber and for your own.

Thus spoke his godfather, and dismissed him from the entrance gates.

VII

The godson went on and on, and as he walked he kept thinking to himself: "How am I to relieve the world of evil? The world relieves itself of evil by sending evil men into exile, by casting them into prison, by executing them upon the scaffold. How, then, will it be possible for me to rid the world of evil without taking upon myself the sins of others?" Thus did he ponder and ponder, yet could not resolve the problem.

On and on he went, until he came to a field in which the corn had grown up rich and thick, and was now ready for the harvest. Suddenly he perceived that a calf had wandered into the corn, and that some peasants, having also seen it, had mounted their horses and were now chasing the calf from one side of the field to the other through the corn. Whenever the calf was on the point of breaking out of the corn a man would come riding up and the calf would double back in terror. Then once more the riders would go galloping about through the crop in pursuit of it. Yet all this time an old woman was standing weeping on the highway and crying out:

- My calf is being driven to death!

So the godson called out to the peasants:

- Why ride about like that? Come out of the corn, all of you, and then the old woman will call her calf back to her.

The peasants listened to his urging, and, advancing to the edge of the corn, the old woman cried aloud:

- Here, here, little madcap! Come here, then!

The calf pricked up its ears and listened. For a little while it listened, and then ran to the old woman and thrust its head against her skirt, almost pushing her from her feet. And it all ended in the peasants being pleased, and the old woman likewise, and the calf as well.

As the godson went on he thought to himself: "I see now that evil cannot be removed by evil. The more that men requite evil, the more does evil spread. Thus it is manifest that evil is powerless against evil. Yet how to eradicate it - I don't know. It was pleasant to see the calf listen to the old woman's voice. Yet, had it not listened, how could she ever have recovered it from the corn?"

Thus the godson pondered and pondered as he went.

VIII

On and on he walked, until he came to a village, where he asked at the first hut for a night's lodging, and was admitted by the goodwife. She was all alone in the hut, and engaged in washing it and the furniture.

Having entered, the godson went quietly to the stove, and stood watching what the woman was doing. She had finished the floor and was now starting to wash the table. First of all she swilled it over, and then began wiping it with a dirty clout.

She rubbed it vigorously one way, but still it was not clean, since the dirty clout left streaks upon its surface. Then she rubbed it the other way about, and cleared off some of the streaks, while making fresh ones. Lastly, she rubbed it lengthways, and back again, yet only with the result of streaking its surface afresh with the dirty clout. One piece of dirt might be wiped away here and there, yet others would be rubbed in all the firmer.

The godson watched her for a time, and at last said:

- My good woman, what are you doing?

- Do you not see? - She said. - I am cleaning against the festival day, but, although I am tired out, I cannot get this table clean.

- But you should first of all rinse the cloth, and then rub the table with it."

The woman did so, and very soon had the table clean.

- I thank you, - she said, - for what you have taught me.

In the morning the godson took leave of his hostess, and went on. He walked and walked, until he came to a forest. There he saw some peasants bending felloes. The godson drew near them and saw that, however much they kept walking round the felloe-block, a felloe would not bend.

So he watched them, and realized that this was because the felloe-block kept turning with them, since it lacked a stay-pin.

As soon as he saw this, he said:

- My brothers, what are you doing?

- We are bending felloes, - they replied. - Twice have we soaked these felloes, and worn ourselves out, yet they will not bend.

- But you should first of all make fast the felloe-block, - said the godson, - and then the felloe will bend as you circle round.

Hearing this, the peasants made fast the felloe-block, and thereafter their work prospered.

The godson spent the night with them, and then went on again. A whole day and a night did he walk, until just before dawn he came up with some cattle drovers, and lay down beside them. He saw that they had picketed their cattle and were now trying to light a fire. They kept taking dry twigs and setting fire to them, yet the flames had no sooner sprung up than they put wet brushwood upon them. The brushwood only gave a hiss, and the flames went out. Again and again the drovers took dry twigs and lit them, yet always piled wet brushwood on the top, and so extinguished the flames. For a long time they laboured at this, yet could not make the fire burn up.

And the godson said,

- Do not be so hasty in piling on the brushwood. First draw up the fire into a good flame. When it is burning fiercely, then put on the brushwood.

The drovers did so. First of all they drew up the flames to a good heat, and then applied the brushwood, so that the latter caught successfully, and the whole pile burst into a blaze.

The godson stayed with them for a while, and then went on again. He kept wondering and wondering why he should have seen these three incidents, yet could not come up with a reason.

IX

For the whole of that day he pressed on, until he came to the forest in which stood the hermit's cell. He approached the cell and knocked at the door, whereupon a voice from within called out to him: "Who is there?

- A great sinner, - replied the godson, - who has come here to atone for the sins of another.

Then an old man came out and asked him further:

- What sins of another are those which have been laid upon you?

So the godson told him all - about his godfather, and the bear and her young, and the throne in the sealed room, and the command which his godfather had given him, and the peasants whom he had seen in the field, and their trampling of the corn, and the calf running to the old woman of its own accord.

- It was then, - said the godson, - that I understood that evil cannot be removed by evil. Yet still I know not how to remove it. I pray you, teach me.

And the old man said:

- Yet tell me first what else you have seen by the wayside as you came.

So the godson told him about the woman and the washing of the table, as also about the peasants who were bending felloes and the drovers who were lighting a fire.

The old man heard him out, and then, turning back into the cell, brought out thence a little notched axe.

- Come with me, - he said.

He went across the clearing from the cell, and pointed to a tree.

- Cut that down, - he said.

So the godson applied the axe until the tree fell.

- Now split it into three.

The godson did so. Then the old man went back to the cell, and returned thence with a lighted torch.

- Burn, - he said, - those three logs.

So the godson took the torch, and set fire to the three logs, until there remained of them only three charred stumps.

- Now, bury them half their length in the ground. So.

The godson buried them as directed.

- See, under that hill, - went on the old man, - there runs a river. Go and bring thence some water in your mouth, and sprinkle these stumps with it. Sprinkle the first stump, just as you taught the woman in the hut. Sprinkle the second one, as you taught the felloes-makers. And sprinkle the third one, even as you taught the drovers. When all these three stumps will sprout, and change from stumps to apple trees, then will you know how evil may be removed from among men, and then also will you have atoned for your sins.

Thus spoke the old man, and retreated to his cell again, while the godson pondered and pondered, and yet could not understand what the old man had said to him. Nevertheless, he set about doing as he had been bidden.

X

Going to the river, and taking a full mouthful of water, he returned and sprinkled the first stump. Again, and yet again, he went, and sprinkled the other two. Now he began to feel tired and hungry, so he went to the cell to beg bite and sup of the old man; yet, hardly had he opened the door, when he saw the old man lying dead across his praying-stool. The godson looked about until he found some dry biscuits, which he ate. Then he found also a spade, and began to dig a grave for the old man. By night he brought water and sprinkled the stumps, and by day he went on digging the grave. Just when he had finished it and was about to bury the old man, some peasants from a neighbouring village arrived with presents of food for the aged hermit.

Learning that the old man was dead, and believing that he had blessed the godson as his successor, they helped to bury the body, left the food for the godson's use, and departed after promising to bring him some more.

So the godson lived in the old man's cell, subsisting upon food brought him by the people, and doing as he had been bidden - that is to say, bringing water in his mouth from the river and sprinkling with it the stumps.

He lived thus for a year, and many people began to come to him, since it had got abroad that a holy man was living the devout life in the forest who brought water in his mouth from under the hill to sprinkle with it three charred stumps. Very many folk visited him, and even rich merchants brought presents, but the godson would accept nothing for himself beyond necessaries. All other things which were given him he handed to the poor.

Thus his order of life became as follows. Half the day he would spend in fetching water in his mouth for the sprinkling of the stumps, and the other half he would spend in resting or receiving visitors.

In time he began to believe that this must really be the way in which it was appointed him to live, and that by this very mode of life he would succeed both in removing evil from the world and in atoning for his own sins.

A second year passed without his once omitting, or any single day, to sprinkle the stumps: yet none of the three had yet begun to sprout.

Once he was sitting in his cell, when he heard a man ride by on horseback, singing to himself as he went. Going out to see what manner of man this was, the godson beheld a fine, strong young man, well-dressed, and mounted on a valuable horse and saddle.

So the godson hailed him, and asked him what his business was, and whither he was going.

The man stopped.

- I am a highwayman, - he said, - and ride the roads and kill people. The more I kill, the merrier is my singing.

The godson was horrified, and thought to himself: "How am I to remove the evil that must lie in such a man? It is easy for me to counsel those who visit me, because they are themselves repentant, but this man glories in his wickedness." However, he said nothing, but went on reflecting as he walked beside the man: "What is to be done now? If this highwayman takes to riding this way he will frighten the people, and they will cease to visit me. What use will it be for me then to go on living here?"

So he stopped, and started telling to the highwayman:

- People come here to visit me not to glory in their wickedness, but to repent and to pray for their sins' forgiveness. You, too, repent if you have any fear of God. But, if you will not, then ride the roads elsewhere, and never come this way again, so that you may not trouble my peace and terrify the people. Should you not listen to me, assuredly God will chastise you.

The highwayman laughed.

- I neither fear God nor will listen to you. - He said. - You are not my master. You live by your prayers and piety, and I by murder. Everyone must live somehow. Do you go on with your teaching of the old women who come to you, but do not attempt to teach me. Yet because you have reminded me of God this day, I will kill two more people tomorrow. I would have killed you yourself this instant, but that I do not wish to soil my hands. For the rest, keep out of my way.

Having uttered these threats, the highwayman rode away. Yet he came no more in that direction, and the godson went on living quietly as of old for another eight years.

XI

One night the godson had been sprinkling the stumps, and then returned to his cell to sit and rest a while. As he sat there he kept looking along the little forest path to see if any of the peasants were coming to visit him. Yet none came that day, and the godson sat alone until evening. Growing weary, he began to think over his past life. He remembered how the highwayman had reproached him for living by his piety, and began to recall his whole life.

"I am not living as the old man told me to," - he thought. - "The old man laid upon me a penance, but that penance I have turned into a source both of bread and of public repute. I have been so led into temptation by it that I find time hang heavy on my hands if no visitors come. Yet, when they come, I am pleased only if they extol my piety! It is not thus that I must live. I have been led astray by the praise of men. So far from atoning for my past sins, I have been incurring new ones. I will go away into the forest - away to some new spot where the people cannot find me, and there I will live entirely alone, so that I may both atone for my past sins and incur no fresh ones."

Thus the godson pondered in his heart. Then he took a little bag of biscuits and the spade, and set out from the cell towards a ravine, in some remote corner of which he hoped to dig for himself an earthen hut, and so hide himself from the people.

As he was walking along with the bag of biscuits and the spade, there came riding towards him the highwayman. The godson was afraid, and tried to flee, but the highwayman overtook him.

- Where are you going? - asked the brigand.

The godson replied that he wished to hide himself in some spot where no one could visit him. The highwayman was surprised at this.

- But how will you feed yourself, - he asked, - when no one can come to visit you?

The godson had not thought of this before, but as soon as the highwayman put the question he remembered the matter of food.

- With whatever God will give me, - he replied.

The highwayman said nothing more, but started to ride on his way.

"What can I be thinking of?" - said the godson suddenly to himself. "I have said not a word to him about his mode of life. Maybe he is repentant now. He seemed softened today, and never once threatened to kill me."

So he called after the highwayman:

- Yet I beseech you to repent, for never can you escape God.

Upon this the highwayman turned his horse, seized a dagger from his belt, and brandished it at the godson, who straightway fled in terror into the forest. The highwayman did not pursue him, but said:

- Twice now have let you go, old man; but the third time, don't appear in front of me, for I will kill you.

This said, he rode away.

That evening the godson went to sprinkle the stumps as usual—and, behold! one of them had put forth shoots, and a little apple tree was growing from it!

XII

So the godson hid himself from men, and entered upon a life wholly solitary. When his small stock of biscuits came to an end he bethought him: "I must go out and search for roots." Yet, hardly had he set forth upon this quest, when he saw hanging from a bough in front of him a little bag of biscuits. He took them down and ate them. No sooner had he done so than he saw another little bag hanging on the same bough. Thus the godson lived on, with no anxieties to trouble him, save one - fear of the highwayman. Whenever he heard him coming he would hide himself, thinking: "If he were to kill me I should die with my sins unpurged."

He lived in this manner for ten years. The apple tree on the one stump grew apace, but the other two stumps remained as they had always been.

One day he rose early, and went out to perform his task of sprinkling the stumps. He had done this, when he felt weariness overcome him, and sat down to rest. As he sat resting there, the thought occurred to him: "Surely I have sinned the more, since now I have begun to fear death. Yet it may be that it is by death itself that God means me to atone for my sins."

Hardly had he thought this, when of a sudden he heard the highwayman riding towards him, and cursing as he came. As soon as he heard him the godson thought: " None but God Himself can work me weal or woe," and so went straight to meet the robber.

Then he saw that the highwayman was not riding alone, but was carrying a man behind him, and that the man's hands were bound and his mouth gagged. The man could utter no word, but the highwayman was cursing him without ceasing. The godson advanced towards them, and stood in the horse's path.

- Whither are you carrying this man? - he said.

- Into the forest, - replied the highwayman. - He is a merchant's son, and refuses to say where his father's money is concealed, so I am going to flog him until he tells me.

And the highwayman tried to ride on, but the god son seized his bridle, and would not let him pass.

- Let the man go, - he said.

The highwayman was enraged at this, and shook his fist at the godson.

- Do you want the same as he? - He asked him. - I promised you long ago that I would kill you. Let me pass.

But the godson felt no fear now.

- I will not let you pass, - he said. - I fear not you, but only God, and God has bidden me detain you. Let this man go.

The highwayman knit his brows, then seized his dagger, cut the bonds, and released the merchant's son.

- Away with you both, - he said, - and never cross my path again.

The merchant's son leapt to the ground and fled, but when the highwayman tried to ride on again the godson still detained him, and told him that he must abandon his wicked life. The highwayman sat quietly listening, but said nothing in reply, and then departed.

In the morning the godson went to sprinkle the stumps as usual—and behold! another one of them had sprouted, and from it a second little apple tree was growing.

XIII

Another ten years passed, and one day, as he was sitting free from anxiety or fear of any kind, and with his heart light within him, the godson thought to himself: "What blessings are given to men by God! Yet they vex themselves in vain when all the time they should be living in peace."

He thought of the vast sum of human wickedness, and how men distressed themselves to no purpose. And he felt a great pity for men. "I ought not to be living thus," - he thought. - "Rather ought I to go forth and tell men what I know."

Just as this had passed through his mind he heard once more the highwayman approaching. At first he was for avoiding the brigand, thinking: "There's no point speaking with this one, he wouldn't understand."

Thus he thought at first, but then he changed his mind, and stepped forth into the road. The highwayman was riding upset, and with his eyes fixed upon the ground. As the godson looked upon him he felt a great pity for him, and, running to his side, clasped him by the knee.

- Dear brother, - he cried, - have mercy upon your own soul, for in you too there dwells a God-given spirit. If you continue thus to torment yourself and to torment others, assuredly worse torments will await you. Yet think how God yearns towards you, and what blessings He has laid up for you! Do not destroy yourself, my brother, but change your way of life.

But the highwayman only frowned and turned away.

- Leave me, - he said.

Yet the godson clasped him still closer by the knee, and burst into tears.

At that the highwayman raised his eyes and looked at the godson. He looked and looked, and then suddenly slid from his horse and threw himself upon his knees on the ground.

- Old man, - he said, - you have overcome me at last. Twenty years have I striven with you, but you have gradually taken away my strength. Now I am not master of myself. Do what you will with me. The first time that you pleaded with me I was but the more enraged. It was not until you withdrew yourself from people, and recognised that you didn't need anything from them, that I began to think over your words. But from that moment I began to hang the bags of biscuits for you on the bough.

Then the godson remembered how it was only when the woman rinsed the cloth that the table was cleaned: even so, only once he had ceased to worry for himself and thus purified his heart, and he had been able to purify the hearts of others.

And the highwayman went on:

- But the first real change of heart took place in me when you ceased to fear death at my hands.

Instantly the godson remembered that it was only when the felloes-makers had fastened firmly the felloes-block that they had been able to bend the felloes. Even so, he saw it was only when he had established firmly his life in God and humbled his presumptuous heart that he had ceased to have any fear of death.

- And, - said the highwayman, in conclusion, - it was when your heart went out to me in pity, and you wept before me, that my own heart was changed entirely.

Rejoicing greatly, the godson led the highwayman to the spot where the three stumps were - and behold from the third stump also an apple tree had sprouted! Then the godson remembered that it was only when the drovers' fire had kindled to a blaze that the wet brushwood had kindled with it. So also, he saw, had his heart within him kindled to a blaze, and with its flame had set fire to the heart of another. With joy he recognised that his sins were at last redeemed.

He told all this to the highwayman and died. The highwayman buried him, and lived thereafter as the godson had bidden him, and taught men to do likewise.

www.ingramcontent.com/pod-product-compliance
Lightning Source LLC
Chambersburg PA
CBHW030710110426
42739CB00031B/1779